the world is young

by wayne miller

a ridge press book

publisher: jerry mason

editor: adolph suehsdorf

art director: albert a. squillace

editorial coordinator: ruth birnkrant

assistant art director: norman snyder

production manager: arthur gubernick

production: allied graphic arts, inc.

printing: r. r. donnelley & sons company

Prepared and produced by THE RIDGE PRESS

551 Fifth Avenue, N.Y. 17, N.Y.

PHOTOGRAPH BY EDWARD STEICHEN

On a summer morning I watched the children playing and once in a while their actions made a picture and I took it. It had been going on like this for about a week and this day one of them finally looked up and said, "Daddy, how much longer are you going to make pictures of us before you go to work?"

That moment three years ago was the real beginning of this book. The idea I had thought about so long and circled about so warily and put aside so often now seemed a clear challenge. The pictures I was taking had a reason and a point: I had begun a photographic exploration of the world of childhood.

A perceptive man once said that "to look at the world through the eyes of another would be true knowledge." This is what I have attempted here. For three years I have tried to look with children rather than at them, and to see through their eyes—and in their forms and faces—the sense and meaning of the experiences that crowd each day when the world is young.

It was not easy. My own children I knew almost too well. Often I found myself straining to overcome conventional, habitual views of who they were and what they did in order to see them honestly and clearly. Other children I did not know well enough. There was always uncertainty whether I could represent them fairly. And, inevitably, I was always myself, never wholly detached, subject always to old prejudices and passions.

Still, in time and as far as I was able, I think I found fairly straight, reasonably uncluttered channels to most of the children you will see. Silently, internally, empathically, I shared their hopes of winning a fight or answering well a question in school, their make-believe thoughts while playing with dolls in houses without walls, their disappointments as they sat alone, trying to understand.

It can be truly said that children created this book. No picture among the many thousands that were taken was intended to support any preconceived point of view. Every one shows only what I understood to be happening at the time. If this were not so, these would not be statements of children that are, but illustrations of children that should or might be.

One time I explained to David, my eldest boy, that he was a combination of inherited and acquired characteristics. Afterward he asked, "But what part of me is me?" I couldn't answer him because I didn't know. Certainly he was asking one of life's bigger questions and one for which each of us, ultimately, must arrive at his own answer. Now I think perhaps this book may offer some clues to David and to other children, too. Perhaps it shows that others often think and feel as we do, that the need to love and be loved is in everyone, that each of us would rather succeed than fail, would rather know than not know.

And as these also are adult concerns, adults may be able to see something of themselves here. Part of each of us is the child we were. To the extent that we hold on to childhood experiences and understandings, there is a child within, living and directing parts of our adult lives. In the children on these pages it may be possible to see and understand who that child might be.

At the start, I thought of many ways this book might be done. I seriously considered attempting a cross section of the world's children. Then I thought a wide sweep through the diversity of the United States might give me what I wanted. But in the end I chose the children and the community I know and understand best. Jeanette, David, Dana, and Peter—the principal children in the book—are my own. They and my wife, Joan, are most important to me. It seemed logical to start the exploration of childhood in our family.

As a family, I think we are in close touch with each other. Joan's attitude as a mother embraces compassion as well as discipline and this has created a warmth of living for all of us that helps keep life's complexities to a minimum. Doing things together as a family—although we don't do as much as we would like—has proved a positive way of life for us. The children seem happiest when we are working as a unit, and as parents, Joan and I have found the children to be good friends.

We live in the unincorporated town of Orinda, California—Pop. 15,000—which sits among rolling hills eighteen miles east of San Francisco. It is a new community without tradition, grandmothers, and, until this year, enough children to make up a senior class in our new high school. Most of us are new settlers who arrived after World War II. The Millers came in 1949. Other families are still coming. We all have some young ones and might have some more.

In this setting, the book begins. The opening pages establish our family. David took the photograph of Dana and me on Page 14 and Joan took all the others in which I appear. We felt the family should have a visible father and I must say that I enjoy being shown as I am. The frontispiece photograph of our family was made by Edward Steichen. This, too, gives me pleasure, as the Captain is a close and meaningful friend to all of us.

Following this is a close look at each of the four children. Each child's section shows him involved in thought and action that seem most characteristic of him, although certainly not unlike that of other children of the same age. Changes in the children reflect, of course, the three-year span over which the pictures were taken. Peter was a child of four when we began, Jeanette a young lady of thirteen when we finished.

Play and make-believe complete this first part of the book.

The exciting and demanding world of school comes next. Here the Millers are not so prominent. You will see them, but they have begun to blend into the society of other children.

Finally, the book ends on the edge of adolescence, where boy-girl relationships take on new meanings and the outlines of life ahead appear.

Once the work began in earnest, my 35mm camera was with me all the time. It was within reach while eating. At night it was beside my bed. When we went shopping or on a picnic or to a program at school, I had my camera, extra film in my pockets, and uneasiness in my gut. I never knew when a picture would form in front of me. I could never be positive I'd seen what I thought I saw. Joan's help in keeping me alert when my awareness lagged was immeasurable.

Aside from the ever-present problem of trying to achieve a child's perspective on the world, I was concerned about the camera-consciousness of my subjects. Would they be distracted by my presence? Could they possibly be wholly themselves with an adult constantly around?

I was not too worried about my own children. Since birth they have been exposed to cameras and have taken photography in stride. Occasionally, pictures occur to them that they would like to try and it is not unusual, when I am developing film, to find strange portraits at weird angles, in-and-out-of-focus pictures of cats, or bands of sunlight coming through flowers. But this time, familiarity with the camera was not enough. To establish a consistent point of view, I would have to be "invisible" to them, as well as to other children. For all practical purposes, when I had a camera in hand I was no longer their father. When a minor accident took place or if they got into trouble, they couldn't look to me for help. They were on their own. Fortunately, nothing ever happened to put this resolution to a severe test.

The family soon understood why I "didn't go to work," but spent all my time around the house and neighborhood taking pictures. With other children, I had some explaining to do. I told them I wanted to understand childhood and that the photographs were for a book. I hoped they would allow me to share their lives and, in return, I would not interfere or pass any judgments. Before long, they too ignored me.

I never talked with the children or reacted to anything they said or did. And while the book was in progress, I never showed them any photographs. I remember a fight one day on a school playground. The teacher in charge went about her business, assuming that I would break it up. I took pictures, wondering why somebody didn't break it up. Fortunately, the bell rang and saved us all.

As I progressed, I found that the closer and deeper I looked, the more I saw and the more there was to see. When I couldn't see any more, the deficiency was mine. I simply wasn't understanding. Sometimes in the swirl of classroom activity, images would swim together and I had to go for a walk and clear my head. On returning, it was possible to see the class again as individuals struggling with individual problems.

With each passing month, I realized that this new world I had entered was boundless and overwhelming in its expression of life forces at work. Before my eyes were fabrics being woven and courses charted that would be with these children to their dying day. Failure, frustration, and defeat, success, pleasure, and triumph were being carved into their natures, together with smells and sights and sounds and things without names. I found the children themselves are very aware of this. Their days are life-size days filled with life-size thoughts. I asked a nine-year-old recently if he'd like to be in kindergarten again and he answered, "Heck, no. I wouldn't go through all that stuff again for nothin'."

When the job was over, it seemed to me that the only people capable of commenting accurately on the pictures would be children. Not every picture situation prompted a remark. Not every emotion revealed could easily be put into words. But from many of these inhabitants of childhood came expressions of extraordinary candor and wisdom. To the watchful eye and the listening ear, children give generously.

I cannot tell at this point what David or anyone else will see in this book. But for me, two things are now certain: each of us is himself and no one else, and each of our worlds is undaunted and hopeful. For all our differences, as one child said, "it's kind of like everybody's got something in common."

The World Is Young

PHOTOGRAPH BY DAVID MILLER

"It's kind of like everybody's got something in common."

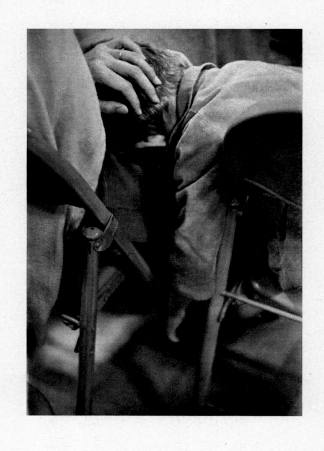

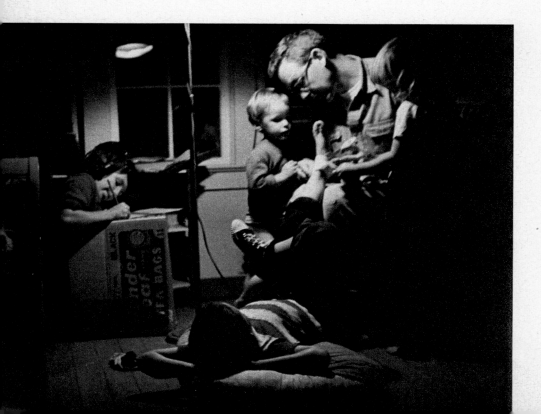

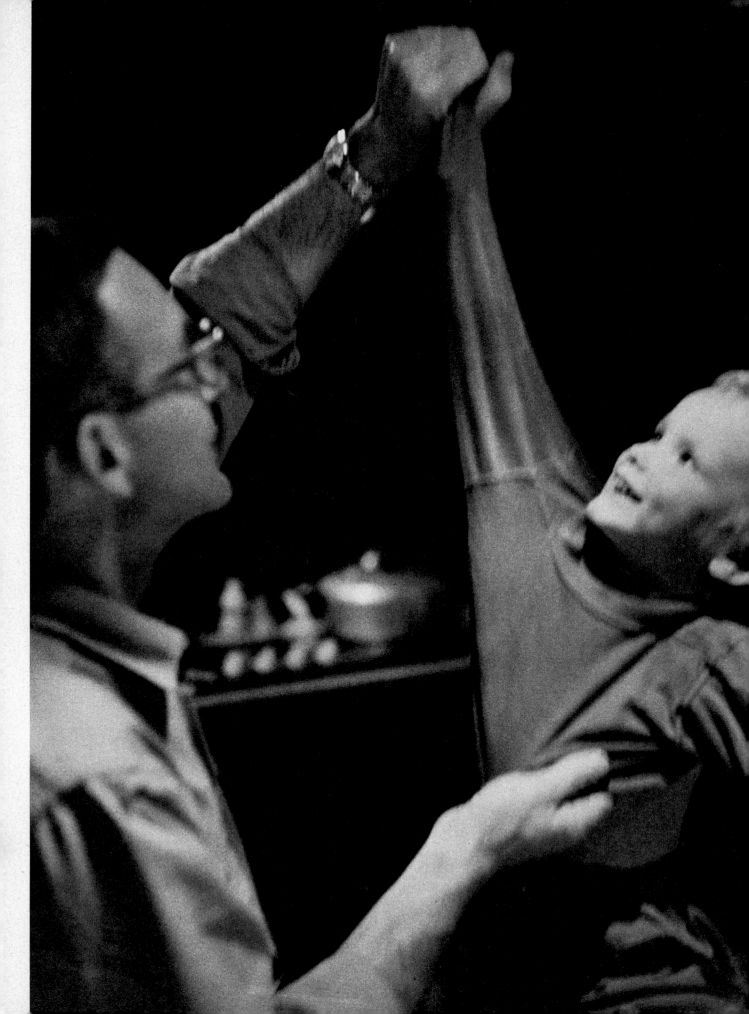

"I'm going to run away and

never come back."

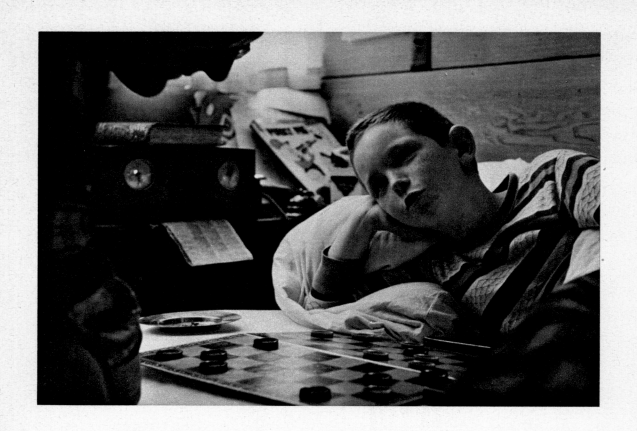

"A boy at our school said, 'Gee, your Mom is nice.

I wish my Mom was like that'."

Peter

"When I grow up, will I be a girl or a boy?"

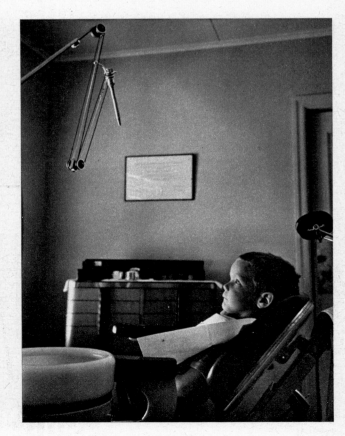

Dana

"Being close to someone means that inside I'm not alone."

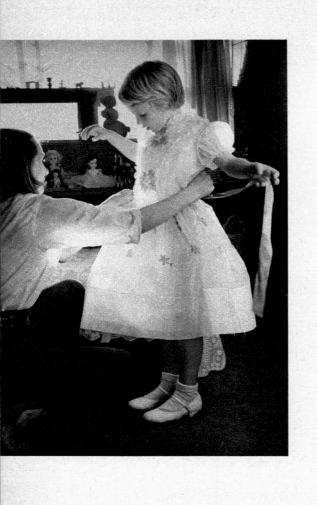

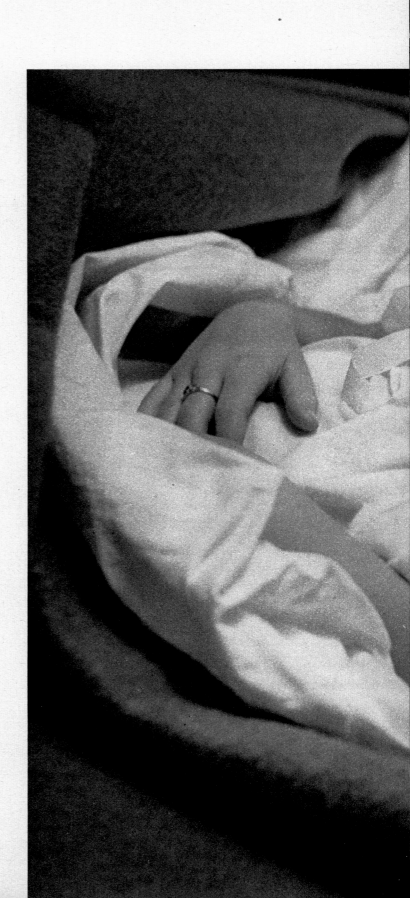

David

"What part of me is me?"

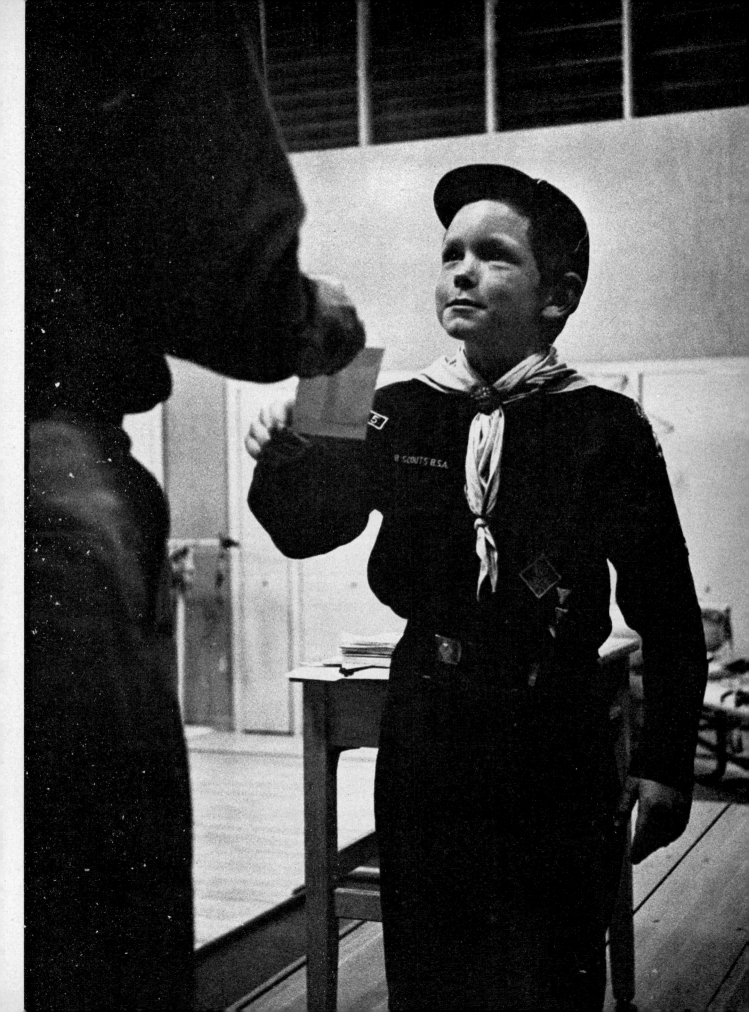

Jeanette

"I wonder."

"I have a secret world of my own, but I don't want to talk about

it because it wouldn't be secret then."

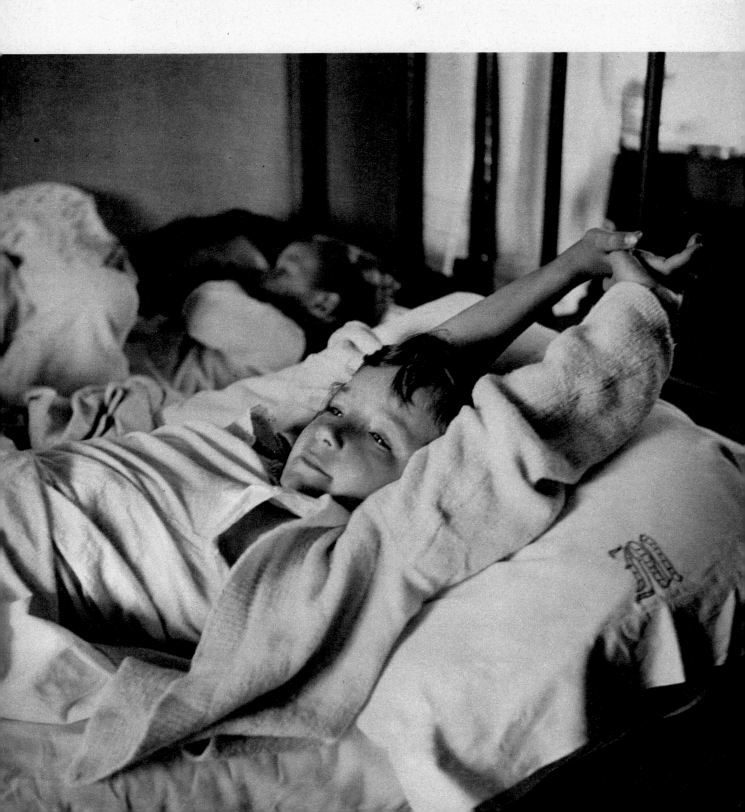

"Next Year"

At the beginning of the school year when Peter was four-and-a-half, the older children were full of talk about school. Peter began asking his mother how long it would be before he could go, too. The explanation "next year" was unreal and unsatisfactory. As the others hustled about each morning, getting ready, Peter sat and watched.

Finally, one morning, he asked that lunch also be made for him. He collected some books and "things to share in class" and put them into a large box with his lunch. When the time came, he left for the bus stop with the others. While waiting for the bus, he shared his books and toys with the other children. The school bus came, picked up its regular passengers, and left. Peter watched it go. After a moment, he sat down and ate his lunch. When he had finished, he carefully put his things back in the box and started his usual morning visits to his neighborhood friends.

"Fun is something you like to do that you can do."

"I like things the way they are."

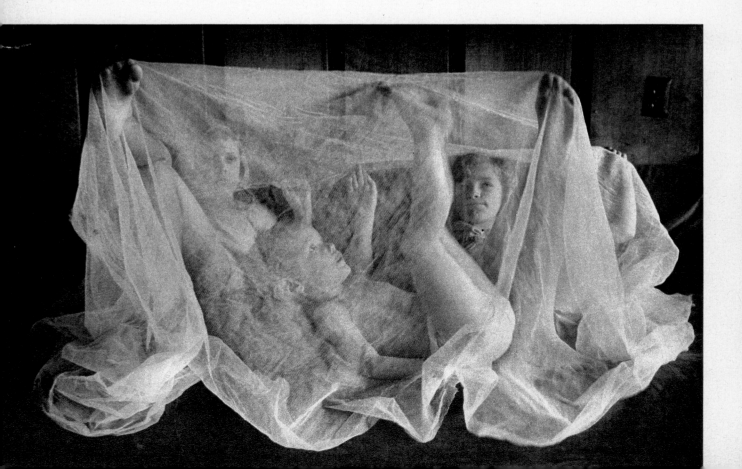

Outside the home there is the beckoning world of other experience and other people. When their time comes, children go forth to make their way with strangers. The exodus is gradual. Days still begin and end in the warm circle of light that is the place where a person belongs. But the impulse, with each new venture, is to go farther afield, to feel the stirring of new responses, to form new certainties and new allegiances.

I cannot prove this. I simply saw it happen.

It began at school. We have six schools in Orinda—four elementary, one for seventh and eighth graders, and a new high school. With the exception of one old-timer, they all are postwar additions to the community, like ourselves. They are handsome, one-story structures of glass, cement, and redwood, and all of them are getting handsome new wings we never thought they'd need.

From all I can see, we have a normal school district. Each school has a mothers' club. Each teacher sees the parents of each child at least twice a year to discuss how he's getting on. And anything the School Board asks for, the parents rush to provide, stumbling over each other in their eagerness to vote "yes" at the polls. The birth rate, however, seems to keep ahead of the bond issues by several classrooms.

For Orinda's children, of course, school life is of vast importance. It fills many hours of their days. It encourages freedom of inquiry and demands the discipline of learning. It deals out the privileges and penalties of being oneself among others.

My interest was to show as many of the children's personal concerns in this setting as I could see and understand. The School-District Superintendent and his staff were very helpful. There were no restrictions. I had free run of the classrooms and school grounds.

At the start, I hung around the playgrounds before and after school, at recess, at lunchtime. "Watcha doin'?" I told them. "What kinda camera's that?" I told them. "Can I see it?" I showed them. "What's he doin'?" He's taking pictures. "Can I see the pictures?" Not now. Maybe later.

I tried to be patient. The questions—thousands of them, I swear—were like drops of water on my forehead, but I answered them. If I could have figured out some way to make myself invisible, I would have done so.

In time, they saw I had a job to do and was serious about it. I became a familiar and unremarkable part of the day. They ignored me and went back to leading their own lives. Once in a while, when I moved in for a close-up, a child became confused and embarrassed, but when I asked him to forget about me and act as though I weren't there, he usually did. Maybe all a person has to do to disappear is to say he isn't there.

Each day and each situation were different. Superficially, there were many elements of sameness in the children's lives. One arithmetic class was much like another, any given afternoon's play was indistinguishable from the rest. The difference came with the overpowering fact of growth. For each growing child, each minute brought change.

The first day in a new situation was often rough until I separated what the children actually were doing from what my older eyes and brain told me they were doing, or perhaps wished them to do. Sometimes things happened too fast for me to catch them. Sometimes the developing moment would dissolve into self-consciousness and disappear. One morning, I remember, was unbearable. I was in a classroom where everything seemed to be popping at once. I saw elation, conflict, vigor, puzzlement, laughter—and I wasn't getting any of it. I shot too late. I shot the child next to the child who was the picture. I was frustrated and irritable and it showed. At this point, the teacher, a kind and discerning person, whispered to me, "They're getting to you today, aren't they?"

A little later, the children had cleared their desks and were waiting for the lunch bell to ring. Either the clock was fast or the bell slow. In those restless moments, the teacher asked questions and stirred up answers, and I caught the class photograph on Pages 100–101.

Other times, without effort on anyone's part, things went beautifully. On the first day of school, one year, I saw a little girl having difficulty leaving her mother. I felt her struggle to enter the newness of first grade and, after mother left, I followed her into class. The other children decided I was a member of the school staff. The teacher, I learned later, thought I was the little girl's father. The pictures are on Pages 90–93.

Pages 96–99 were the result of another hunch. These were taken on the first day of a summer-school program that offers special courses not given during the regular term. When the first bell rang and the other children entered their classrooms, one girl hung back. The look on her face and the lines of her body showed her conflict clearly. I wasn't sure she'd make it. But the courage to decide was in her. Turning to her mother, she said, "I can go by myself."

A basic viewpoint of the book was established almost by accident. I was photographing kindergarten children one day when a fifth-grader hove to, bearing a message for the teacher. Beside the tiny kindergarteners, he was a giant and I was suddenly struck by the knee-high view little children have of the life around them. From then on, all pictures were taken from the subject's eye level, so that the people and things around them would be seen in a proper context. There are few "little" children in the book. They are all full size, life size, their size. The best proof I had that this was the right approach came on the playground one day during a Maypole program. I was on one knee making photographs when a pre-schooler came over, threw his arms about me and kissed my cheek. Being on the same level, I decided, creates understanding.

I am not a child psychologist, and I had no wish to see profound significance where it did not exist. Watching these children as closely as I did for three years, however, I saw much that seems genuine to me, and that prompted me to snap the shutter when I did.

Recess, I found, was a time of changing status. The bright boy who had led a classroom discussion with sure skill now might find himself on the edge of the crowd while more agile classmates chose up sides for football. It was not only a matter of muscle. For some it was simply not knowing how to make contact or how to assert themselves in the energetic disorder of the playground. One of these quiet ones said, "At recess, I just go out and watch." And a girl who knew the feeling said, "You want to get away from people. You just stand there and you just watch people do things."

Some of my conclusions are after the fact. They were formed when the job was done and I studied the many moments fixed on film and saw patterns and textures I hadn't realized were there. The evidence of the pictures shows, for instance, that rough and violent play is for younger boys. Girls join them only when the pace slows down a bit. In Fifth and Sixth Grades, boy groups and girl groups may be side by side, but the play is separate. (See Page 113.) The balance seems to come in organized activity—folk dancing, plays, the band or orchestra.

Formal organizations—Cubs, Brownies, Boy Scouts and Girl Scouts—seem to be a source of pride in being linked with a larger effort. Of Cub Scouts, a boy said, "We do things together. Wearing the uniform is a sign that we're all together." Friends are introduced as being "in my Den" and boys encountered around town are identified as "in my Pack."

"In Sixth, you get down to business," I was told. Stiffer homework, more demanding classroom work, maturing bodies, and new boy-girl awarenesses bring pressures as well as pleasures. The sixth-grade children I photographed were considered an exceptional group. They worked well together. Their spirits were always high and they had an extra eagerness to learn. The class had more than its share of leaders in all fields—scholastic, athletic and social. It made me feel good just to be with them. I followed them throughout the three years and it may be that you will recognize some of them as they grow up toward the end of the book.

In Sixth, happiness was heaven, failure the end of everything. The girl on Page 128 had received good news: although her class was being broken up and she was moving to another school, a much-admired teacher would still be with her. The discouraged girl on the opposite page had not been able to finish an arithmetic test in the allotted time.

As you look at Seventh Grade, you know that life is now more real and earnest. "You don't play jump-rope in Seventh," one boy told me with dark finality. And he is right. Seventh graders look different and act different. If you crouch in a classroom aisle with a camera and watch these new persons finding new difficulty in reciting before the group, you know that the carefree younger grades are now far behind and feel a twinge of adult sympathy for what's ahead.

Both seventh and eighth graders are aware of the importance of being successful in the eyes of their classmates. Success means many things, but most importantly it is personal success, or better yet, being a successful person. Standards and boundaries to be tested arise on every side. Goals to reach appear on the horizon.

They are thinking children and they find the words to express their new views of adults, of their developing selves, and of the future. "I wish my parents would understand me like kids my own age do," says one. "Sometimes I feel grown up," says another, "and sometimes I feel lost." "I'm excited to go ahead, but scared because I don't know what will happen," says still another.

But for all their doubts, they are determined people. "All of a sudden, you're a new person," one of them told me. "I want to go on."

Next Year

When "next year" did arrive, Peter didn't say much about school, but happiness radiated from him like sunbeams. When the family awoke on the day that school began, Peter was all dressed and waiting. He was the first to leave the house, the first to show off his new shoes, first in line, and the first one on the school bus. This was his day.

His enthusiasm lasted three days. The fourth day, he didn't want to go to school at all.

Kindergarten

"Look at me."

First Grade

"But, Mommy, I don't have any friends here."

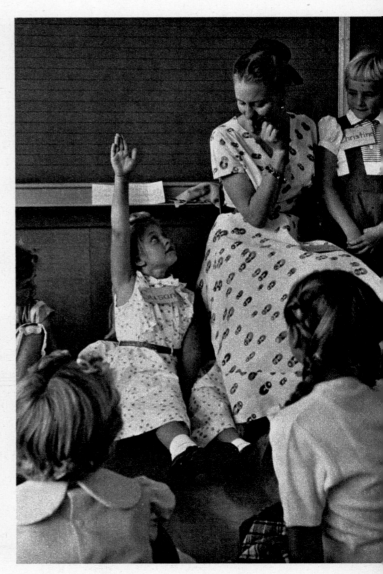

Second Grade

"I can go by myself."

Third Grade

"*First you push the damper in,*

"*Then you pull the damper out,*

"*And the smoke goes up the chimney just the same.*

"*Just the same,*

"*Just the same,*

"*And the smoke goes up the chimney just the same.*"

SINGING AND RHYMING
GINN AND COMPANY, 1950

"I am a tree."

Fourth Grade

"If the teacher is interested and wants you to learn,

you have more interest in your work and what she teaches you."

"At recess I just go out and watch."

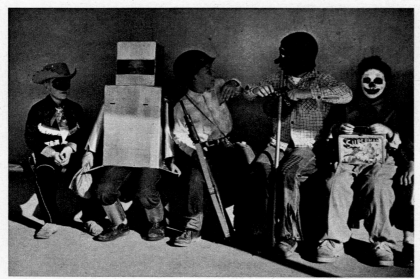

"I want to be different."

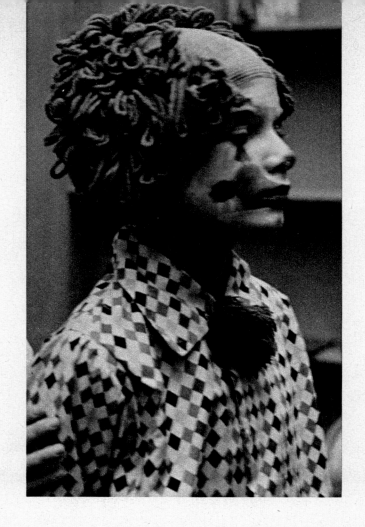

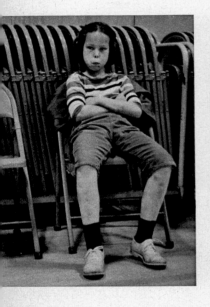 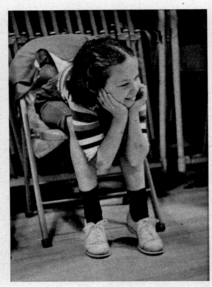 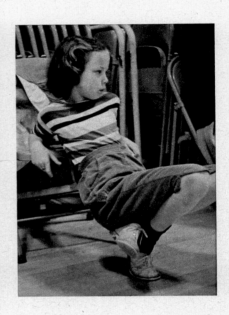

  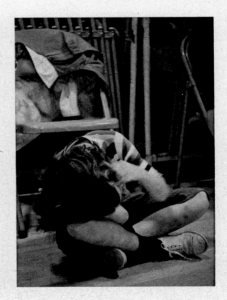

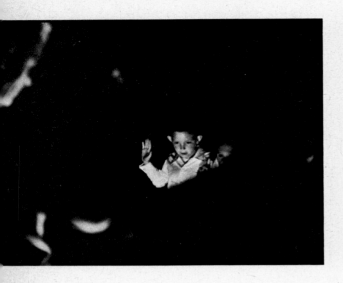 

"You learn to work

and have fun together."

Sixth Grade

"You feel like you're growing up."

"In Sixth, you get down to business."

"There's no sense in knowing something when you don't understand it."

"You feel bigger when you're on the best team. Because you are

the best. It gives you a feeling that you are the best."

AIR-RAID DRILL:

"You wonder if
you're going to die."

Seventh Grade

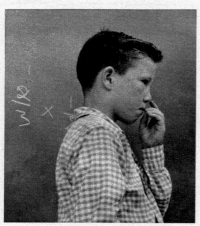

"They tell you to act your age and when you do they get mad."

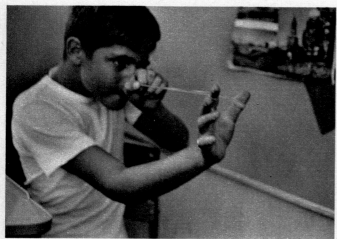

Now the end of childhood is in sight. In many ways the young people who conclude this book still are childish or childlike, but less and less are they children. "You feel a sudden strongness," says a graduate of Eighth Grade, "because you can think for yourself." "There's a difference," says another. "Your dreams start to mature. You go your way."

Yet the way is not easily found. Nor is the search for it easily described. Although children are now more vocal—you will find more picture comments here—even words and a willingness to use them cannot tell it all. For the theme of these final pages is the awakening emotions that will sway the mature body and give purpose to the developed intellect. And this is an area where one person interprets another only tentatively and with great care.

From what I saw over the past three years, nothing important happens quickly. The wish to know one another starts early and never really ends. The affectionate interest these children are beginning to take in each other is built on a past of making friends and fighting with friends and on all the hard lessons of learning about oneself that lead to understanding others. Eventually, a person knows enough and has enough to want to share himself with others.

The early boy-girl parties are variations on schooltime activities. These are overt and boisterous. Then, quietly, for one child and then another, come awarenesses that create self-consciousness. "Why do people always look at me?" a child may cry with dismay. But curiosity restores the balance; gossip and close scrutiny of others become a major concern. I noticed that by about Sixth Grade the schoolyard contained three groups: active ones playing games, lone watchers, and—by far the largest group—talkers. They talk about other children, about teachers, parents, themselves. Sometimes they listen.

The experts might not agree with me, but I also felt that most of the fighting I saw was a desperate, roundabout effort to make friends. One boy, especially, seemed often to get into fights when he attempted to join children playing. Through his tears, he has said, "Why won't you let me play with you? I don't have anyone else to play with." He is also the boy who said (Page 146), "It never seems to work out when three guys want to play together."

As for girls, the feeling is that "they don't get mad very often." They don't hit each other much, I agree. But they do lay on with strong words. "I hate you, I hate everyone, I hate everything," I heard one howling. Afterward, and cooled down a bit, she said: "When you're angry, you don't know what you're doing. You're angry and you blame everybody for this and that, and maybe you think you did the right thing, but you didn't."

Smoldering criticism of parents becomes more frequent. "You don't understand!" is the recurrent cry. "They give you adult responsibilities and treat you like a child," says one. And, "if you're not treated as a grown-up, how can you act like one?" Teachers "tell you to act your age, and when you do they get mad."

The un-understanding parent also seems unfair. One afternoon David came to Peter's rescue during a fight over a tree swing and found himself disciplined by his mother for being the attacker (Pages 150–151). He was sent to his room feeling, with righteous indignation, that "it isn't fair!" A boy who saw the pictures later said with sympathy, "Boys don't argue back, but they *think* back." "When she's bawling me out," said another boy thinking of home and mother, "I think all the bad things about her that I can."

By Sixth Grade, many girls are vibrantly alert to boys. This is clear. They primp,

they wear more petticoats, they tease and chase boys. In my ignorance, I asked why. The girls looked appalled. "Girls chase boys to catch them."

Boys are too busy "just doing things" to notice. At parties they roughhouse and do handstands and act timid about dancing. Girls frequently dance with each other. Girls occasionally acquire "boy friends." They go steady for a week or two at a time. The girls are quite concerned about these relationships, but the boys seem unaware of their new responsibilities.

By Eighth Grade, however, the tables are turned. The boys tease and chase the girls who quite enjoy being caught. As one boy said, "They do something to you and when you do something back it's a way to have fun." Outside of school, "you go places and meet people and you hope the right girl is there." At dances, the boys now do make choices and the girls are pleased at being chosen. Those who go steady believe that "when you go steady, you're accepted by the whole crowd and then you've got it made." Those who don't aren't so sure. They say, "It isn't that important."

These children have their beginnings behind them. Their experiences and

understandings have begun to shape their lives. At first hesitant, they now are moving forward. Boys who were, collectively, "a great big nuisance" turn out not to be, after all. The uncertainty of "I don't want to grow up" becomes the confidence of "You think for yourself." This forward movement, this going on of the mind and body, is the story of childhood. In time, each young person slowly and almost imperceptibly departs childhood. Welcoming life as it is and as it will be, one child said, "It's happening like it should be happening."

"We went steady for around a week."

"All the girls talk about the boys and all the boys talk about the girls."

"I hate you,

I hate you,

I hate you."

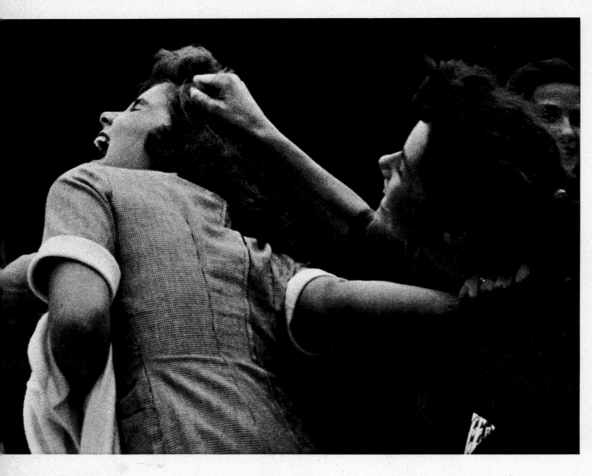

"It never seems to work when three guys want to play together."

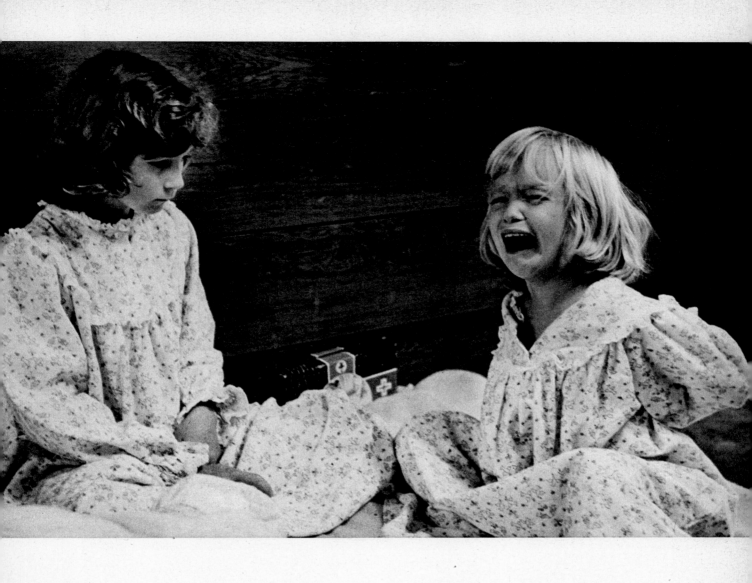

"It isn't fair."

"When she's bawling me
out, I think all the bad things
about her that I can."

"But you don't understand."

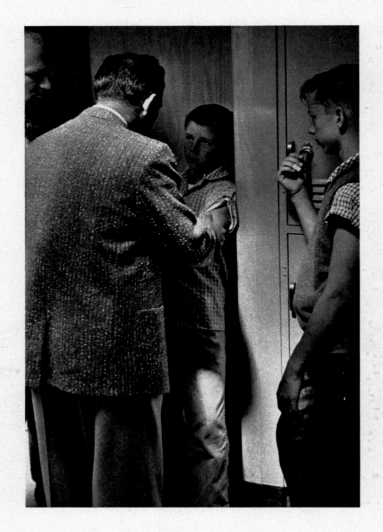

153

"I'm your friend."

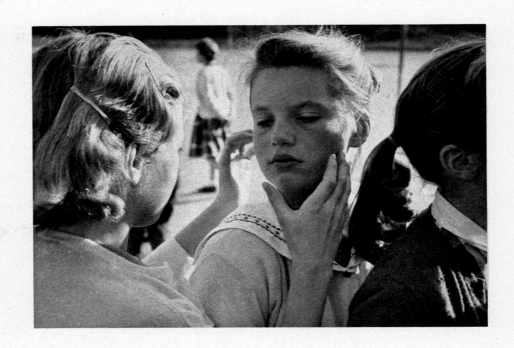

"I feel alone inside."

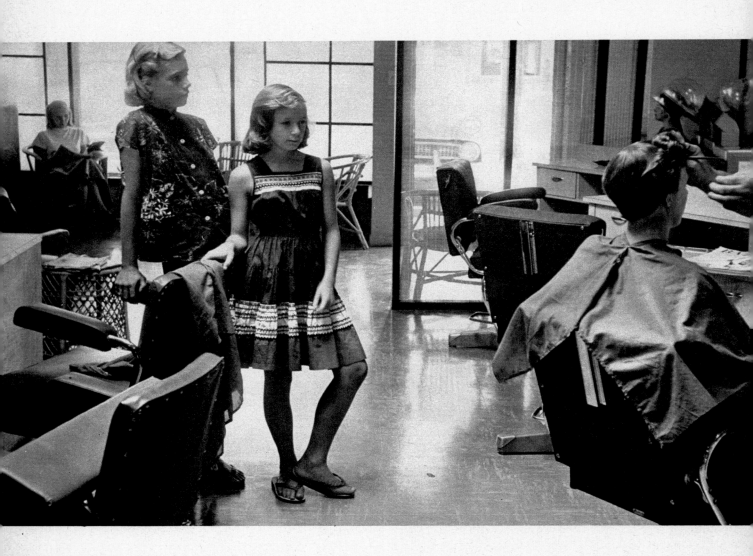

"I don't like boys. I think they're just a great big nuisance."

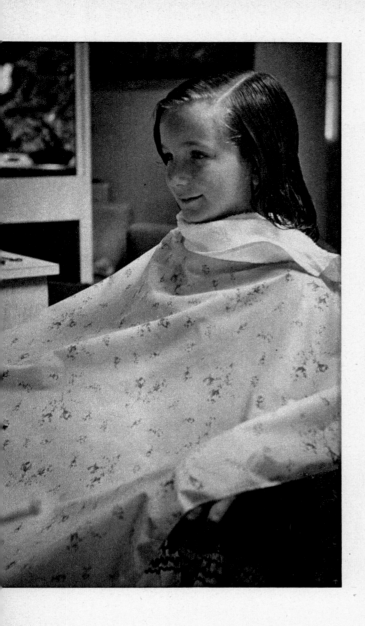

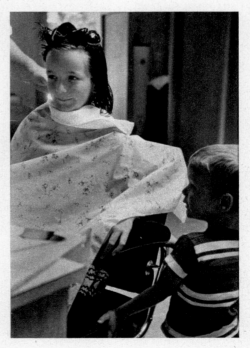

"All of a sudden,

it's something new."

"Girls chase boys to catch them."

"It's conversation without talking."

"Girls become a bigger and bigger subject."

"When you first kiss a girl, it's so new that it gives you

a feeling that you want to do it more and more."

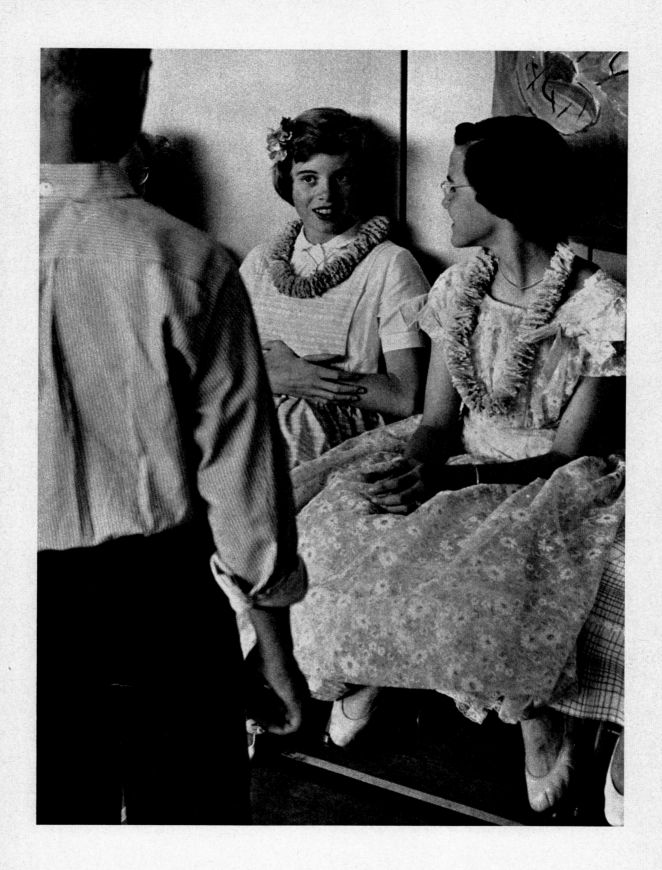

"It's happening like it should be happening."